D1614330

The Phoenix Living Poets

A PINT OF BITTER

A
PINT OF BITTER

by

ALAN BOLD

CHATTO AND WINDUS

THE HOGARTH PRESS

1971

Published by
Chatto and Windus Ltd
with The Hogarth Press Ltd
42 William IV Street
London WC 2
★

Clarke, Irwin and Co Ltd
Toronto

ISBN 0 7011 1691 9

© Alan Bold 1971

Printed in Great Britain by
William Lewis (Printers) Ltd
Cardiff

And for the future — (but I write this reeling,
Having got drunk exceedingly to-day,
    So that I seem to stand upon the ceiling)
I say — the future is a serious matter —
And so — for God's sake — hock and soda-water!

Byron, *Don Juan*

for BARRY COLE

*— prose for elegant exposition
poetry for emotional precision*

CONTENTS

Iris, Messenger of the Gods

On a recent trip to Paris, from London by night,
I thought I'd do some "Reflections on Woman".
As the boat moved, girls' faces grew more white,
Lovely jaws sagged, and normally tight
Muscles slackened bizarrely, hardly human.

In the Tuileries, by the pond near la Concorde,
I saw three female generations, the hips
Were the clues — straight, curved, and blurred —
And I was obsessed by the sounds that slurred
From the oldest, scooping with her gallic lips.

Then to the Rodin Museum, rue de Varenne,
I headed, for an hour or so of art,
Watching flesh more than bronze, when
I saw *Iris Messager des Dieux*, and women
Avoiding her — because she keeps her legs apart.

9

My First Sweetheart

You were the *belle* of the street
And very conscious of it.
You were a shade richer
Than everyone else and knew
In your bones you were better
Than those of us who danced
Outside your main door,
Coming from flats, where
Darkness was thicker
Than thin air, so you stood
Outside the grand door and let
Us have just a squint inside.
You never deigned to play with us,
Displayed inordinate pride,
Mocked our clumsiness,
Our coarse voices, our
School uniforms labelling us
As lesser beings than you.
But I loved you and
I didn't understand what love was
For or how you did it.
I just loved you, and
I wonder if you remember
A valentine that had on it
The outline of a hand,
A pink water-colour wash,
And the words "I love you"
Written all over it?
I sent that. I posted it
Myself and walked past
Your house for a sign
That you had seen it
And had understood.
But nothing happened.

10

The world didn't suddenly become
Marvellous for me, my life
Didn't really alter. So
I'll remember you in
Your golden ringlets, in
Your party dresses
That I saw sometimes passing
By your house. Your
Plump cheeks will always
Signify something transcendental
For me. I wonder what became
Of you when you left the street,
Left me without anything substantial
To dream about, with your house
Become a bed-and-breakfast place.
The light steps that took me round
The corner to see you became slow
And I scuffed my satchel in the
Leaves as they gathered outside
Your door. But it wasn't the same
Without you. You must have
Been the same age as me.
Seven or eight or nine.
Still, I don't think anyone
Has ever been so mysterious.
Of course, we'll never meet.
These things never really happen.
Perhaps just as well.
Though I wonder what would
Have happened if I had just once
Come and pulled your bell
And said: "Hello, I love you."

One Way of Closing

I followed the figure that had crossed my path
Down a narrow lane, and then beyond.
Night merged with day, country with town,
Nightmares swirled, daydreams screamed down.
Then, with his feet skirting a still green pond
I saw, mocking my own form, the figure of death.

It was so dark the incandescent sun
Hung like a hazy bulb in the utter gloom.
I tried to speak, but the grinning face now stared,
And one long finger pointed and prepared
Me for some ordeal. Suddenly a tomb
Was ready, gaping open for someone.

Butterflies and bats, fireflies and birds,
Swooped about the structure, made it hard
To desire to enter anywhere but there, yet
Beneath the stone enclosure the muddy pit
Stung into my eyes until I barred
My soft intentions, strengthened them with words.

With piercing laughter pinching at my ears
I screamed and tried to frighten my unwanted host,
Demanded to go further than the earth, said
Only a lighter prospect would see me dead.
Tried to win an argument over this vile ghost
But reluctantly succumbed, drenched in my own tears.

Something Happened

the central hall was massive
   scalloped with battered gold
and inside was to feel smaller
   a corpse in the earth's cold

the rich jewelled ceiling
   shrunk as the whirring stopped
the water all around us
   turned to ice as it dropped

the fleshy blood-stained entrance
   oozed around like sperm
the young ones grasped each other
   clasping close to keep warm

a thundering hammering spluttered
   as red as the sky was grey
and we watched them move in silence
   to hear what they wanted to say

the gestures carried nothing
   created their own surprise
and the sense of sinking increased
   as they grew before our eyes

the last thing I remember
   was a crushing glance of doom
as they seemed to cover everything
   seemed to become the room

the central hall was massive
   scalloped with battered gold
and inside was to feel smaller
   a corpse in the earth's cold

13

B

Circular Song *(for Robert Thallon and Brian Bell)*

(In my eyes there's a clear
Little rivulet of fear
As I see you dissolve
As I watch you disappear.

You intend to depart
Then to make another start
But the feelings are bad
Like the pressure on my heart.)

I'm not holding on to these long pauses
Or serving time as one of your lost causes
I'm concentrating on the certain choices.
   I've taken everything
   The mud that you could sling
   And at this space of time
   Want to wash off the grime.
I've had a basketful of come-back letters
And paper stiffens into hard hard fetters.

You use me as a passport to high places
To drool and throb at all the well-bred faces
You'd love to know exactly what the pace is.
   But it's a losing game
   For me you're still the same,
   Too selfish by a whole
   Division of my soul.
So now you'll listen when I say I want no more
And am content to let you draw up your own score.

When I'm there
You'll still say no,
But when I leave
You never seem to let me go.

I'm not the answer to your bright daydream
Some application to melt with your face-cream
Can't keep on crying like any old spring-stream.
    So drop the telephone
    Let me be on my own
    Forget you knew of me
    Be what you need to be.
Perhaps when older you will lose these clutches,
But for the present I know what too much is.

It's quite an elegy for someone leaving
I won't pretend that you don't leave me grieving
But then by going I am really giving.
    It is a farewell song
    I'm not where you belong
    You'll find, with your scent,
    Somebody permanent.
This is the last time I will think about you
And as I've told you, you must do what you have to.

15

On the Seventh Day

Sad as longing, active as water,
The harbour stirs slowly on Sunday.
The trawlermen stare or aimlessly potter
With nets and ropes and pine away.

Far from the fish they feel unwanted.
Everything appears lazy and slow.
Hands clasped behind them, haunted
By the huge persistent urge to go.

Perhaps a new arrival has the harbour-master
Down in the van, or a foreign boat
Swaggers in, going straighter and faster
Than normal, as the home fleets float.

Over the water wood bobs around
And the sun blindingly glitters on the sea.
Still the fishermen make hardly a sound
Watching the water enviously.

Tomorrow they will go and then complain
Of the cold, and they will wait and wish
For the shore, as the nets wrench pain
From their hands, these foragers for fish.

The Day I Committed . . . .

. . . . . . suicide even those
Who most disliked me gladly rose
To drink a solemn glass of beer
And wish, fond wish, I was still here.
Men who thought me mad or worse
Now spoke of me, and no curse
Accompanied their discourse.
The word spread fast and piety
Became the order of the day.
The day was dull, appropriately,
It had everything, except me.
The buses slammed along and kept
A place reserved for those who wept
Openly, were overcome with grief;
The newspapers, to their relief,
Had something palpable to write
And dropped obligatory spite.
Critics who thought my verse abstract,
Scientific, matter of fact,
Now saw that it was sensuous
And shed real tears over "this bitter loss
To letters". And the very books
That once had earned me filthy looks
Were hailed as works of literature
Pointing to a great future.
"No one left to fill his place",
Was written in a special place
(Written as if deeply meant)
In *The Times Literary Supplement.*
All papers, by proprietorial order,
Came out with a black-edged border.
They interrupted the weekly sport
On television with a shock report
Of my demise, and the way I died.

17

Housewives all over Britain cried
On learning of my suicide.
In Downing Street the Prime Minister
Held his mourning wife and kissed her,
Motored to a press conference,
Determined to insert some sense
Into the hysteria sweeping the nation,
But even his high station
Could not stop a manly sniff
Breaking from him. A large stiff
Whisky (they used my favourite brand)
Helped to steady his trembling hand
And he emerged before the press
Almost controlling his distress.
"Gentlemen", he cautioned, "we must strive
To keep the country's strength alive
Even amid catastrophe.
Remember the great history
Of this unique small country
Try to deal with tragedy
As boldly — O I'm so sorry —
As bravely as I am sure he,
Now sadly gone, would agree
We should. I feel, you see . . . . "
But great thoughts of the newly dead
Pumped the blood into his head
And as he battled with his brain
He ordered a large scotch — again.
"How", one reporter queried,
"Will we battle through another period
Of economic restraint without
His presence. Personally I doubt
If anyone can give the inspiration
He did in *The State of the Nation*.
To put it bluntly, can MPs

Without new volumes on their knees
Possibly follow policy
Or represent their constituency
In the absence of his sacred works?"
"That way danger lurks",
The premier replied. "I can
Assure you that the National Plan,
To coin a phrase, will survive
As it would were he alive.
Remember that we have to bind us
The word of Messrs. Chatto and Windus
That a new edition of *The Poems*
Will be placed in all our homes,
Biblically bound and sprayed with gold
Embossed with the legend Alan Bold . . ."
But at the name confusion burst
Out once again, and first
To calm himself was the great
Leader of the state.
"I'm sorry, but I must insist
This conference closes. We have missed
A great man today but his spirit
Will continue to guide the cabinet.
I want the whole country to know
That we can recover from this blow."
But, just in case, I'm making sure
The country doesn't lose this vast treasure.
Knowing that everyone was so kind
I'm glad to say I've changed my mind.

Departure

A dress, a book, a yellow vase
Drag around like people when she goes.
Not any but the ones she chose
   Talk to me now
   Instruct me how
Much my world is the world she has.

Travelling sometimes I see the sky
Uncertain if it's real or a mirage.
Seems then I need the personal touch
   To make it real
   To make me feel
A part of the blank sea that swamps my eye.

Tried to make my life one pose
Indifferent to this girl or the next.
Comes to it I'm the one who's axed
   Pushed here and there
   Out of her care
And in my guts a toxic flower grows.

Graffiti

i

Instead of singing of unrequited love
Make with the women. You'll be better off.

ii

The last words of Shaw: 'I'm going to die."
You'd think even a deity would wonder why.

iii

I see vast monuments to The Glorious Dead.
May I have the price of my brick now, instead?

iv

Chip shop. An old man dying in grease
To hear you saying: "Ninepence worth please."

v

I drink to forget, but whenever I think
I'm happy I rejoice in drink.

vi

To triumph over creativity is the critic's hope,
But who do we remember: John Dennis or Pope?

vii

In my own age-group I've never had the luck
To shock anyone with words like "fuck".

viii

The difference between Man and the ant.
The ant does what he can, Man what he can't.

ix

I try to get the warts-and-all even when I paint
Myself, but always become a persecuted saint.

x

The sky has turned from Bonnard-blue to pale Picasso-pink.
Which means you don't see colours now. You merely think.

xi

I cannot really sympathise with those
For whom philosophy is expressed in clothes.

xii

Aristocrats. Bourgeoise. Proles.
All divided by assuming roles.

After a Debate
(for Michael Grieve)

From Aberdeen to Edinburgh, I
Travelled on a train from a debate.
(The anti-Scottish feelings and the hate
I poured on Scotland forced me on to try

To win the motion and demonstrate why
All things Scottish could only create
A little anti-England not a state
Of independence.) Now what of his reply?

Thus I watched the rough grip of this land
Its rugged tight embrace. I wonder how
I missed the landscape in my argument.

And on the sweep of Scotland I will stand.
I could not love it more, and even now
Concede the whole case to my opponent.

Dance Suite

1

First the way the fingers flutter
Then the rhythms placed, at once,
Every movement seems to matter
As the muscles move in dance.

Messages melting like a lover,
Statements filtered silently,
A language wordless forever
And momentous as this day.

Formal freedom, static fury,
Face and feet and form and fun,
As the limitless story
Moves as only motion can.

2

Out there in the darkness millions of stars
Blink out their light that reaches us now we
Exist in superfluity of wars

And dance grotesquely in a parody
Of natural movement that is destroyed
By each acceptance of normality

So totally abnormal in the void
We spin in (though we act at being still
Assuming variations have been tried).

Absolutely wrong: it is the will
To move, to dance, that motivates this earth,
The wonderful pavanne the daffodil

Performs that makes its growth and colour worth
So much attention, or the brisk gavotte
Of grass, the pattern that no human birth

24

Could do without, the swaying and the beat
That is the pulse of life, the burst that blood
Creates in regular impulses hot

And thick and energetic as the thud
That drums against the heart in dark red pools
That thump, a massive tom-tom that we would

Die to dismiss; the dance of molecules
And dance of entropy, of everything
That contributes toward the dance that rules

Each sacred moment. And our bodies sing
Silently in the pursuit of dancing.

3

Astonishing images suggest themselves, sustain
Themselves only intermittently, then prove evanescent
As the butterfly, given flight cruelly for an instant
In our life, which is an instant in the life
Of the earth, which is as nothing in the grand-scale
Movement of the galaxy, and thus the face, the dance,
Immortalise our aspirations precisely for the moment
That we have them, then fade before finality
Destroys their definitions, and the subtle tones
That rush as shadows on a twisting darting head
Promise further secrets, impress on the watcher
The mystery that is expressed schematically
As the quality that transcends the purely functional
Physiological structure of the species. This
Is the dance, this is the effort
That liberates in orgasmic instantaneous
Ritualised irrationality.
And there is the constriction of clothes
Mundane jobs mortgages credit payments
Contributory pension schemes superannuation

And the attrition of professional bitchiness
Working constantly on the consciousness
Numbing it, reducing it to a simple reflex
Of vicious hostility. This
Is the enemy of the dance.
What there is positive is attacked
What creative ignored
What graceful and vital and essential
Ridiculed
And dancing through a heat haze
Of alcohol and simulated laughter
And arbitrary friendships contracted,
Like the consequences, for the night.

4

As each message from the future starts
Glancing in, the senses stir and see
The objective light of history,
The visual ululation that departs

The instant it arrives, then our hearts
Are eras older for the ecstasy
Of observation and the tragedy
Of dying is reduced to beating parts.

The clumsy jerking we began with blends
Into a sensuous surge of bodies sweet
With dancing, with the fusion and the grace

That masters the limitations that space
Imposes on its contents, and we meet
In motion opening our empty hands.

Open Letter

How this gentle rush
In my brain, my heart,
    Makes me push
Back, towards the start.

And to reinact
The first twist of love
    As I cracked
Could not give enough.

I recall the taste
But will not repeat
    How I raced
To the indiscreet.

And this must be hard
That other men hear
    What we shared
What it meant too, dear.

Words are not a way
Of explaining you
    Just to say
I adore you too.

The Solution

Even after the shadows had renounced
Their secrets before the gorgeous golden haze
That seemed to span the sky, there were still
Questions that the world had violent days
To formulate. The fastest made their kill
With ease and, as their bodies pounced
On slower, weaker mammals, they regressed.

Tumbling on itself the sphere moved space
Through light and dark and colours bloomed
As plants diversified and lids drew back
To look at them, while the eyes were doomed
To see their own container only in a lake
Or river where the ripples flawed the face.
But the creature saw itself and was obsessed.

With an image of itself the creature closed
The eyes, and, with a thought like thunder,
Wanted every thing in its own likeness. It saw
The other animals with cautious wonder
At this time, then with contempt as awe
Gave way to anger viciously imposed.
Only the impossibly identical could pass the test.

All the alien species classified
As such were branded and abused
As ornaments or slaves. Over this
The heavy creature that had bruised
All flesh around it destroyed the grace
In other things that subsequently died.
And the creature laughed in the lake, alone at last.

Changes

To see the branches lost in the warm rays
Of summer sunshine is to know the pull
Of love, to linger in the shade where cool
Protection lets me visualise your face

Your body and to dream and always praise
The goodness in you, and the way that you'll
Reciprocate my loving. As a rule
I don't confess, but I have changed my ways.

An open field is worth more than a gun
And structures are not worthy of the name
If they deny to those who live without

The chance to intermingle in the sun
With those within and languish in the same:
Since loving you I have believed in doubt.

Anniversary

I first met love on a dark evil street
    Distinguished by no name.
I wished to scuffle in the murk and meet
    Someone to do the same.
And all the guilt would sweetly sweep us through
    What things we had to do.

The second meeting saw me travelling
    A distance that increased
Whenever the horizon seemed to sing
    And thus was colour teased
Into an almost stark orgasmic blue
    Where only sounds were true.

A last and swift encounter made me stop
    Expecting a device.
So the world's riches swelled to drop
    And others appeared wise:
They had forseen what I could not construe
    Until I married you.

The House in the Distance

The blanket on the rooftops
   Was a blanket of fine snow,
The house in the distance beckoned
   And she knew she had to go.

The house in the distance beckoned
   She knew it was for her,
And she stumbled through the deep white drift
   Cold in her coat of fur.

She passed before the garage
   Choked at the petrol smell
Blushed in her breasts at the talk of the men
   Who scrutinised her well.

She had no idea who was in there,
   That house that stood alone.
From the TV spokes and the curtains
   It looked like Home Sweet Home.

Under the lamp she rested
   Thought of her lovely legs
Thought, "If he wants all this he can pay
   And only if he begs."

"If he wants my thighs to stroke and bruise
   If he wants my breasts to kiss,
If he wants to remove my underthings
   He can pay up for all this."

Her breasts were beautiful and firm
   Her legs were long and slim
Her hair was like a rush of gold
   Her buttocks plump and trim.

31

A servant ushered her indoors
    Then to a vast bedroom
And said, "Wait here, my lovely,
    The master will be up soon."

Mirrors covered all one wall
    The others were thick with jewelled
Swords and scabbards and weapons
    Delicately tooled.

She looked at one of the mirrors
    Shaking her golden locks
Studying her own curvature
    When startled by three knocks.

She looked straight at the large door
    Startled by three knocks,
And gasped at the length of the key he used
    Fastening the three locks.

"My pleasure, honey baby,"
    He said as he came near,
"Is to pay you as much as you want if you
    Promise not to leave here."

"As much as I want?" she asked him.
    "How much can you afford?"
"That, my dear, is determined by me
    And this ceremonial sword."

The sword came out of its scabbard
    And plunged into her soul
And the snow dripped scarlet and the night
    Winced at the endless howl.

Echoes

Now as the black terns move
   Let us move too
Let us fall back in love
Now as the black terns move
As they divide above
   Spraying the blue
Now as the black terns move
   Let us move too

Good Advice

"Turn up the records
    Drown in canned beer
Spin out the worn words
    Talk but don't hear.

Treat every woman
    Like a good lay
Think of your living
    In terms of pay.

Piss on your neighbour
    Covet his wife
Sexual vigour
    Defines the good life.

With enough money
    Buy what you want
Each in his own way
    Has his amount.

Suck the bum's boss
    Toady like hell
Net what you gross
    And all will be well.

Calculate how much
    Friends make each week
Look for the soft touch
    Smile when you speak.

Reach for your stengun
    At the word art
Bring up your son
    To re-play your part.

Good guys get nowhere
   Act like a sod
Broadcast your prayer
   To your equal, your God."

Football Triptych

1
European Cup Final, Lisbon, May 25, 1967
Celtic v. Internazionale Milan

The shot by Chalmers put us one goal up.
Lisbon knew the Scottish side were best.
And Celtic won the European Cup.

Cappellini fouled by Craig, the grip
Of tension put the players to the test.
(The shot by Chalmers put us one goal up.)

Mazzola's penalty made our heart stop,
But now the Celts attacked without a rest.
And Celtic won the European Cup.

Sarti put some rockets over the top,
Yet Gemmell's goal had an unequalled zest.
The shot by Chalmers put us one goal up.

Then Gemmell gave a dance, a little hop,
Murdoch, Chalmers: Inter's chance had passed.
And Celtic won the European Cup.

McNeill crushed forward, held the trophy up.
Jock Stein was laughing as we drank a toast.
The shot by Chalmers put us one goal up.
And Celtic won the European Cup.

2
Jimmy Johnstone

See him swerving on the ball
Perfect balance, armed with all
Athletic graces. Now he shoots,
The ball spins from his magic boots.

36

He has been compared to men
Twice his age, then half again.
Morton, Matthews, Georgie Best,
Dixie Dean — you know the rest.

But who has quite his dribbling powers,
His ability to run for hours?
Who can match, for sheer control,
His motives as he moves for goal?

3

World Cup Final, Wembley, July 30, 1966
England v. West Germany

The might of England shook the Wembley grass
But Germany's Haller was first to score.
A mere two minutes later Bobby Moore
Taking the free-kick made a perfect pass

To Hurst who equalised. And when the mass
Of England-chanters saw their Peters floor
The German keeper, how the Wembley roar
Exploded! Winning by a goal, it was.

But in the dying minutes Gordon Banks
Failed to stop Weber's erratic shot.
In extra time the goals were scored by Hurst.

The first was controversial and was cursed
By every German, but the next was not.
England had won. The crowd gave Ramsey thanks.

Chance Encounter

It was one of those clumsy meetings. It was
Concocted in a sad little coffee bar, and he,
Wet with nowhere to go, came in and sat down.
He had enough for one coffee, one roll, but
Spurned the roll because it dripped grease
And made him queasy. Any Sunday morning
Is something, but this was something special.
Instead of artificially redundant pubs, simulated
Displays of darkly sinister goings-on at church,
Guilty good-mornings, half-averted eyes
With tiny lanes of blood, there was,
On his part anyway, a desire to show dissent
Against the silent day as it dawned
With drizzle and a descending mist.

It was dark enough to be depressing, light
Enough to make him loathe the doing
Of another day. As the waitress passed
He felt a slight tug of desire, but nothing
More. The sugar was like clotted sand
As it plopped in the ugly liquid. The
Clock said six. It had been a long, a
Tiresome journey. It was one of those
Clumsy meetings.

   She hugged her handbag,
Saw the sign, desired to drink.

   "Cold, isn't it?", the waitress said,
Cleaning now, condescending to the solitary
Customer. It took him by surprise,
This voice. "Yes, isn't it."

Her first thought was of money.
She had enough for a week, but a week
Of what? To see the city. To learn
Enough to see the sights of the city.
She had heard how cynical they were,
How much they charged in a coffee bar.

He saw her coming in. She was tired,
Obviously tired, rebuking his self-pity.
There was, on his part, anyway, a desire
To show dissent against the silent day,
But his limbs languished, and his meek
Expression signified a lack of fire
In his personality. If it was sunny,
Ah, but what to do about the weather?

Her hands were cold and she clutched
Her coffee. He noticed how she looked
Around for an empty table, when all the
Tables, save his, were empty. "Sit
Here," he said. "Thank you," she
Answered. "Thank you very much."
She must mistake him for a soft touch,
He ruminated. She bought a cooked
Breakfast, and he with the remnants of
A bacon roll. "Have you just arrived,"
He asked her. But her mouth was occupied
With sausages and egg. "I've just come
From the north." Then he tried
Another angle. "Have you anywhere
To stay?" She stared at him with a hint
Of moral indignation, as if to say:
"If you think you can pick me up in this
Dump, think again brother." But her words
Were: "No. But I hope to find something

39

Today." "So do I." And then they
Both returned to silence for a while.

She finished, said with a smile,
"I have to go, been nice talking
To you. I have to go now." O,
He gestured. "Ah," he said,
But when she rose he did so too.
"Mind if I walk a bit with you?"
She tossed her dark brown curls
And shook her head. Walking
They said little, looked at bridges
In the reddening sky, watched
Seagulls gliding through the air,
Held hands at last. It was
One of those clumsy meetings. No
Bars were open, but they went
To a hotel. She paid for a pint
Of bitter for him, and a vodka
And lime for herself. He had made
His lack of money clear. She
Assumed this was normal for the city,
Didn't mind the company, it was
Better than walking on your own.

The long lazy river that cut up
The city met them at every turn.
There were boats, stragglers, men
In old coats, old newspapers, oil-marks,
Drifting along to the rhythm of the
River, lapping along with small
Secret sounds. Though the smell
Was heavy, the sight was often pleasant.
They had a meal, an outing on a boat,
And there on the river the colour

Came into her face where a pallor
Had obtained before. She was tired,
Both of them were tired. From
Time to time he watched her long legs
That tapered from fleshy thighs to
Athletic ankles. And the breasts bulged
Beneath a shiny raincoat. He was dressed
In grey. But, he thought, they didn't
Make a bad couple. He was impressed.

Coming off the boat they delayed things
Around the docks. It was inevitable.
They spoke in gestures then. He fumbled
For her flesh beneath the clothes. She
Gasped a bit and held him close,
And the sun surged through her tender body,
And the moon whirled in her lovely legs,
And he felt the old familiar passion,
And struck her more than once, until
She fell. He hadn't meant to do anything
At all. Not this time. It had simply
Happened. She was still attractive, crumpled,
And he noticed her knickers were red,
The colour that seeped from her temple
As she lay spreadeagled and dead.

Encore

I am a sullen bugger
    Make no mistake.
Prefer football to rugger
    Like a jazz break.

I am a boorish bastard
    After a drink.
Chunder stuff like custard
    Sickly, I think.

Only good thing in me
    And this is true,
However awful I appear
    I'm no worse than you.

TRANSLATIONS
from the French

The Old Tramp
('Le vieux vagabond', by Jean-Pierre de Béranger, 1780-1857)

Let me finish my days in this ditch.
End them all old, broken, weary.
They'll say I'm drunk as they pass, which
Is fine. They shall not pity me.
I see some turn their heads away,
Others tossing coins, but I
Say: Scatter! Feast yourselves and play.
An old tramp does not need you to die.

Yes, I'm dying here of my decay.
People don't really starve to death.
Hospital, I thought, would make misery
Bearable as I took my final breath.
But the Full-up signs in every poor-house greet
Me. Poor folk are wretched, worn.
The only nurse I had was the street.
An old tramp would die where he was born.

As a young man I didn't shirk.
I asked tradesmen to teach me a trade.
"Get lost, we don't have that much work,
Go and beg for a living," they said.
You rich ones, advising work, I've had
Your leftovers, and could have eaten worse.
Your straw has given me a decent bed.
An old tramp doesn't leave you with his curse.

I could have stolen, being poor, but no.
I preferred to extend my hand.
At most I've clutched the ripening glow
Of an apple plucked from someone's land.
Yet twenty times, by order of the king,
They've stuck me in the dungeons at his whim.
And robbed me of my only precious thing.
An old tramp feels the sun belongs to him.

Does the poor man have a country?
What do I care for your wheat
Your wine your glory or your industry,
Your orators assembled for debate?
When the foreigner arrived and grew fat
Within the walls fallen to his will,
Like a fool I shed tears over that.
An old tramp found his food acceptable.

Why didn't you have me crushed
Like an insect of the filth-carrying kind?
Or, better still, trained and rushed
To work for the benefit of all mankind.
Sheltered from the adverse weather
The maggot might become an ant.
I would have loved you as a brother.
An old tramp, dying, finds he can't.

Correspondences
('Correspondances', by Charles Baudelaire, 1821-1867)

Nature is a temple where living columns
Sometimes let loose their confused rumbles.
There man must pass through forests of symbols
That scrutinise and know him as he comes.

Like long distant echoes that coalesce
In a secret and profound unity
Vast as darkness, immense as the day,
Scents, colours, sounds all answer in congress.

There are perfumes as fresh as children's skin,
Pungent as oboes, green as meadows,
Others rancid like triumphant sin

With the potential Infinity knows
As amber, benjamin, musk, incense is
Chanting the abandon of mind and senses.

Spleen
('Spleen', by Charles Baudelaire, 1821-1867)

I am like the monarch of a rainy country,
Rich but impotent, young but in decay,
Who, sickened by the cringing of his tutors, wastes
His time in boredom with his dogs and other beasts.
Nothing can enliven him — games, falconry,
His people lying near his balcony to die.
His favourite clown's most bawdy ballad cannot make
Any transformation in one so cruelly sick.
His bed, adorned with fleur-de-lys, becomes his tomb
And those admiring ladies who attend the room
Cannot reveal enough in titillating dress
To stimulate a smile in this young carcass.
The alchemist who makes his gold is not equipped
To shift the element whose substance is corrupt.
Even those baths of blood, like those the Romans used,
Have been helpless to heat up that dull corpse in whose
Limbs not blood but Lethe's green water flows.

Get Drunk
('Enivrez-vous', by Charles Baudelaire, 1821-1867)

Always be drunk. That is all: it is *the* question. You want to stop Time crushing your shoulders, bending you double, so get drunk — militantly.

How? Use wine, poetry, or virtue, use your imagination. Just get drunk.

And if occasionally, on the steps of a palace, a grassy ditch, in the bleak loneliness of your room, you come to, your drunkenness diminished or gone, ask wind, wave, star, bird, clock, everything that turns, that sings, that speaks, and ask the time; and wind, wave, star, bird, clock will reply: "Time to get drunk! Rather than be the martyred slave of Time, get drunk perpetually! Use wine, poetry, or virtue, use your imagination."

Sea Breeze
('Brise Marine', by Stéphane Mallarmé, 1842-1898)

The flesh is weary. I've read all the books before.
Escape. Get free. The birds look tipsy as they soar
Drunkenly in the air between foam and the skies.
Nothing — not old gardens reflected in the eyes —
Can keep this heart from drenching in the sea, O nights!
Nor the feeling as my solitary lamp lights
Up unused paper whose whiteness intimidates
Me. Nor the young wife suckling what her love creates.
I shall depart. Steamer, as your rigging bends
And sways, pull up anchor for more exotic lands.

An empty boredom broken by failure tells
Us we need handkerchiefs for the last farewells.
And perhaps the masts, inviting the thunderstorms,
Are those a gale splinters into the broken forms
Of ships lost from rich islands where they would belong . . .
But O, my heart, hear the sound of the sailor's song!

The Hands of Jeanne-Marie
('Les mains de Jeanne-Marie', by Arthur Rimbaud, 1854-1891)

Jeanne-Marie's hands are powerful,
In the summer they get tanned,
They are, like dead hands, pale.
— Is this a lady's hand?

Do they draw their dusky cream tones
From the seas of sensuality?
Are they drenched in moons
In the pools of serenity?

Have they drunk in the atmosphere
While they rested unafraid
On pretty knees? Rolled a cigar
Or dabbled in the diamond trade?

At the zealous feet of Madonnas
Have they flung golden flowers?
Is it the black blood of belladonnas
In their palms that sleeps and glowers?

Do they guide the diptera
Struggling through the bluish dawn
Towards the nectar?
Do they help the poison down?

O what dream has gripped them
In pandiculation?
An unprecedented dream
Of Asia, Khenghavar or Zion?

— These hands have not sold fruit
Or been scorched at the feet of gods:
They have never washed out
The garments of babies with closed eyelids.

51

These hands don't belong to a cousin, or
To working women with big brows
Burnt with a sun drunk on tar
Rising from forests stinking of factories.

These are the moulders of the spine,
Hands that never put a finger wrong,
More inexorable than the machine.
As for the horse: twice as strong!

Smouldering like furnaces,
Dismissing all their fears,
Their flesh chants the Marseillaise
But no religious scores.

They will wring your necks, you evil
Women! Noblewomen, their might
Will smash you hands we still
Relate to carmine and to white.

The radiance of these hands of love
Turns the heads of the sheep;
On their sweet division the sun above
Places a ruby to sleep.

A mark on the people makes
Them brown like yesterday's breasts;
And it is there on their backs
That every rebel's kiss rests.

Beautifully they whitened once
The sunshine of revolt warmed
The metal of machine-guns
Through Paris as the people armed.

Ah, there are times you sacred fist
When chains of shining links
Weep on your wrist
As our lips drip with drinks.

And, angelic hands, there is a strange new
Impulse in us when they try
To strip the sun from you
And make your fingers bleed and cry.

The Peasants
('Les paysans', by Émile Verhaeren, 1855-1916)

These men of the soil, those Greuze romanticised
In the pale colours of the rustic scene,
So sprucely dressed and ruddy, we're not surprised
They make a pretty pattern among the saccharine
Of a Louis-Quinze pastel-pampered salon, yet
They are dull, coarse, brutal — all of that.

They stick together as if the village were a pen.
The people in adjacent market-towns are feared
As aliens, intruders, sworn enemies, men
Fit to be cheated, fooled, devoured.
Their country? Come off it! Which one respects the state
That arms their children to defend its lands?
They see nothing of their mother earth in that,
The earth they fertilize with their hands.
Their country? Deep in their fields they remain
Indifferent to it. What attracts these folk
Is a vague image of a man of gold, say Charlemagne,
Sitting in the fringed velvet of his cloak.
All the pomp of swords and crowns hanging
Escutcheoned on the panelled palace wall,
Guarded by soldiers — tasselled sabres clanging —
This is their idea of power. And that's all.
Otherwise their wits, dull on finer points,
Would clump in clogs through duty, right,
Justice, liberty — instinct slows their joints,
A squalid almanac gives them intellectual light.
And if they faintly hear the roar
Of revolution spreading from the town
They remain slaves in human conflict for fear
If they rebelled they would be brutally put down.